THE NEED TO KNOW LIBRARY™

EVERYTHING YOU NEED TO KNOW ABOUT THE RISKS OF MARIJUANA

DR. SANDRA GIDDENS

Rosen YA™
New York

Dedicated to Dr. Owen Giddens, Dr. Tony George, and JACS organization

Published in 2020 by The Rosen Publishing Group, Inc.
29 East 21st Street, New York, NY 10010

First Edition

Library of Congress Cataloging-in-Publication Data

Names: Giddens, Sandra, Dr., author.
Title: Everything you need to know about the risks of marijuana / Dr. Sandra Giddens.
Description: New York : Rosen Publishing, 2020 | Series: The need to know library | Includes bibliographical references and index.
Identifiers: LCCN 2018045820| ISBN 9781508187684 (library bound) | ISBN 9781508187677 (pbk.)
Subjects: LCSH: Marijuana abuse—Juvenile literature. | Marijuana—Juvenile literature.
Classification: LCC HV5822.M3 G496 2020 | DDC 362.29/5—dc23
LC record available at https://lccn.loc.gov/2018045820

Manufactured in the United States of America

CONTENTS

INTRODUCTION

Marijuana use is a controversial topic that gets a lot of attention and debate from all age groups. The subject is being discussed throughout the media, from television to newspapers to websites, and through numerous chat lines. According to a June 2018 National Institute on Drug Abuse (NIDA) survey, by the time teens graduate from high school, about half of them have tried marijuana at least once in their lifetime. This survey also indicates that after alcohol, marijuana is the second most commonly used illegal substance among students in grade twelve.

In the United States, thirty states allow marijuana for medicinal use and nine states have passed laws to allow recreational marijuana over the age of twenty-one. In 2018, Canada has made legal both medicinal and recreational marijuana for people over the age of nineteen. In 2017, the US marijuana industry had nearly $10 billion in sales. New Frontier Data, a firm that focuses on the marijuana industry, forecasts that legalizing marijuana could produce more than $132 billion in federal tax revenue for the United States in the next decade. Companies are seeing big opportunities for profit in selling marijuana. The beer industry wants to get into the action by making alcoholic drinks mixed with marijuana. Energy drink companies want to make a nonalcoholic marijuana drink. It appears that everyone wants to get into this lucrative game.

Recreational marijuana use has been legal in California since June 2018, allowing residents of the state to buy the drug at dispensaries like the one shown here.

The big question remains: Does marijuana use put teens at risk physically and emotionally? According to the NIDA study, there is research showing that marijuana can be very bad for the development of the brain. It can affect one's schoolwork. It can lead to other drugs. It can lead to addiction. It can be harmful to one's social life. NIDA also suggests that long-term, heavy marijuana smoking can have serious side effects, especially when young people start smoking often and early.

Learning about marijuana will answer some of the questions that young people may ask. They then will have the ability to be more knowledgeable in making better and safer decisions about their lives.

CHAPTER ONE

WHAT DO WE KNOW ABOUT MARIJUANA?

Marijuana is a mixture of the green and brown shredded leaves, seeds, stems, and flowers from the cannabis plant. There are two subspecies of the cannabis plant. One is *Cannibis sativa*, known as marijuana, and has psychoactive (mind-altering) properties. The other plant is *Cannabis sativa L* and is known as hemp. It is not mind-altering and is used for manufacturing oil, cloth, and fuel. The cannabis plant grows wild and can be grown in almost any climate. All forms of *Cannabis sativa* are mind-altering drugs that contain more than four hundred chemicals. The main active chemical is THC (delta-9-tetrahydrocannabinol). THC is the active ingredient in the marijuana plant that gives one the "high" feeling. This chemical is found in resin mainly from the female cannabis plant. There are both male and female marijuana plants but only the female plants produce flowers or buds that contain a usable amount of THC. Marijuana is a drug that can be smoked or eaten in order to create the feeling of being high. When smoked, marijuana has a distinct pungent, identifiable smell.

Female flowers of the marijuana plant grow in spiky clusters and produce THC, which causes those who use the drug to feel high and has both physical and emotional side effects.

People benefitted from making medicines from the cannabis plant a very long time ago. Archaeologists discovered marijuana in digs in Asia that date back to the stone age, 4000 BC. In Asia, the plant was used for medical and spiritual purposes. The illegal recreational drug use of marijuana began when it came to the United States in the 1900's via Mexico.

The popularity of marijuana has ebbed and flowed over the past century. Despite being outlawed in several states in the early 1900s and being criminalized in 1937, marijuana became popular in the 1960s. The 1960s was a time when young people rebelled

The Grateful Dead, shown here in 1975, has been a band closely associated with marijuana use since its start in the 1960s.

against society. They did this through how they dressed, their music, and the abundance of drugs, especially marijuana. Marijuana was readily available. It became a symbol of hippies and counterculture. Marijuana has continued to gain in popularity throughout the United States. According to the 2018 National Survey on Drug Use and Health (NSDUH), of the 27.1 million drug users surveyed, 22.2 million of them reported that they used marijuana in the past thirty days. The survey concluded that marijuana was the most widely used drug in the United States.

CANNABIS, MARIJUANA, POT, WEED

Cannabis has many names, like marijuana, weed, pot, grass, Mary Jane, ganja, dope, joints, and reefers, to name just a few. The reason the plant has so many nicknames is because it has been illegal for ages.

A MARIJUANA TIMELINE

- 4000 BC Archaeologists discovered cannabis in digs in Asia.
- 1700s Farmers were legally required to grow hemp as a staple crop in the United States for production of rope, sails, and clothing.
- 1900 Mexican immigrants introduce recreational use of marijuana to United States.
- 1937 Marijuana Tax Act criminalized marijuana.
- 1960s Marijuana use becomes popular in the media.
- 1970 The Controlled Substances Act prohibits marijuana for any use, including medical, at the federal level.
- 1986 President Reagan signed Anti-Drug Abuse Act.
- 2012 Colorado and Washington become the first two states to legalize the recreational use of marijuana.
- 2014 The US Justice Department allows recognized Indian tribes to grow and sell marijuana on their lands.
- 2017 Gallup's annual poll shows 64 percent support for legalizing marijuana use in the United States.

Having these different nicknames became an underground coded language to keep users from getting caught by the police.

When people use marijuana, THC and other chemicals travel through their bloodstream to their brain and this causes the feeling of being high. Feeling high is described as experiencing a feeling of being extremely

CBD oils are used in medical marijuana. Although CBD does not give the same high as THC, there is a lack of long-term data on its safety and effectiveness.

happy, excited, relaxed, and carefree. Some people do not get the positive high, but get a negative reaction. Their heart rates increase and they can feel anxiety and fear.

The amount of THC in marijuana has continued to increase over the years. The ingredient of the marijuana plant thought to have medical benefits is called cannabidiol (CBD), and unlike THC, it has not increased in strength over time. Some strains of marijuana are being bred to maintain a low THC content and provide medical relief with the use of CBD.

Today's marijuana plants are grown differently than they were in the past. People have become more experienced at growing the marijuana plant to make the strains have higher THC levels. The plants can contain up to three times more THC. Exposure to higher THC levels has been responsible for more harmful reactions in people.

Adults who smoked marijuana in the seventies and eighties would not have the same experience if they started smoking now. Today, marijuana is much stronger.

MARIJUANA, THE BLUNT TRUTH

There are many ways to use marijuana. Many people smoke marijuana in hand–rolled cigarettes called joints. They also smoke in pipes and water pipes called bongs. A blunt is an empty cigar that is filled with marijuana and is also smoked. Smoking liquid or wax marijuana in an electric cigarette or pen is known as vaping. Marijuana can be extracted into oils and made into marijuana tea. There are THC crystals that can be snorted through the nose. There are those who eat raw marijuana. Some people mix marijuana in foods like brownies, candies, or cookies. Kif Kat is a pot-infused candy. It looks like a Kit Kat chocolate bar. Marijuana-laced gummy bears look like regular candy gummy bears. People have to eat more of these edibles so they can get a faster high, and this can lead to dangerous side effects. There have been incidents when toddlers have been rushed to the hospital after accidently eating edibles laced with marijuana.

Marijuana candy, like the pops shown here, can contain several times the recommended adult dose of THC and, if consumed, can be life-threatening to children.

Adults may think when they were teens and they smoked marijuana they turned out fine, so they may believe that today's teens should be just as fine as well. But the higher THC content is more dangerous.

MEDICAL MARIJUANA

Marijuana use with a doctor's prescription is called medical marijuana. Many of the stories about the success of medical marijuana are anecdotal. Medical marijuana is used in a number of forms. Topical medications are lotions, balms, and oils made with medical marijuana that are absorbed through the skin for the relief of pain. Swallowing capsules that contain marijuana oil are another form of medical marijuana. More than two hundred marijuana-based natural health products are authorized for sale. People have said that medical marijuana is helpful in relieving nausea and vomiting, especially when a person is undergoing chemotherapy. People with multiple sclerosis have reported that the drug has relieved their muscle spasms. Medical marijuana has been reported to increase people's appetite if they have difficulty eating because of their illnesses. People who have chronic pain, especially neuropathic (nerve pain), have said that they have experienced some relief when taking medical marijuana. There have been cases of people who have epilepsy and medical marijuana has reduced their seizure activity. In September 2018, the *National Post* reported that medical marijuana has lead to the reduction in the use of opiates.

Many patients report both significant pain relief and a reduced dependence on medication when using medical marijuana, but the medical research is still ongoing.

There is very limited research supporting the use of medical marijuana. In most states that allow medical marijuana, the marijuana is not regulated and therefore is not checked for ingredients, purity, strength, or safety. Doctors prefer scientific researched evidence of a drug. Marijuana, for medicinal reasons, is not the first choice that doctors will recommend. There are alternative FDA-approved medications now for the proposed uses of marijuana. Medical marijuana has become a drug that is self-reported to benefit even without the scientific evidence to back up the reports. Family doctors are prescribing medical marijuana reluctantly as they get increasing pressure from patients asking for it.

The debate over the benefits of medical marijuana is still ongoing. Although it has been approved in many states, it still continues to be a classified controlled substance. Those in support of legalization believe that marijuana offers a safe and effective medical treatment. Those that oppose legalization argue that people are ignoring the harms of marijuana. They feel that the supporters want the approval so marijuana would be easier to obtain for recreational purposes.

THE HIGHS AND LOWS OF LEGALIZATION

In the United States, the use and possession of marijuana is illegal under federal law. Marijuana is a Schedule 1 substance. This means it has great possibilities for misuse and no accepted medical use. Policies regarding the medical and recreational use of marijuana can vary from state to state. In the many states that have legalized marijuana, this conflicts with the federal law. In 2018, Attorney General Jeff Sessions announced that he would allow US attorneys to decide whether to enforce federal laws outlawing the use and sale of marijuana in states that have legalized the drug.

In 1986, President Reagan signed the Anti-Drug Abuse Act, which ordered prison sentences without parole for people who were convicted of selling and possessing illegal drugs, including marijuana. In October 2016, the *New York Times* reported that arrests for possessing small amounts of marijuana were greater than those for all violent crimes. Legalizing marijuana is starting to change people's thinking of such harsh sentences for people possessing marijuana. On September 12, 2018, the *New York Law Journal* reported that Manhattan district attorney Cyrus Vance Jr. moved to dismiss more than three thousand open warrants for low-level marijuana convictions.

The black market has made a huge profit over the years selling marijuana illegally. Having marijuana illegal has cost the United States billions of dollars in lost tax revenues. Legalizing marijuana could help regulate the marijuana industry. People would know the ingredients in the marijuana they purchase such as how much THC was contained in their joint. Americans' support for legalizing marijuana continues to rise in most age groups. But taking an illegal drug and making it legal requires careful study and independent research.

CHAPTER TWO

THE RISKS OF RECREATIONAL MARIJUANA

There is ongoing research on the effects of marijuana on young people. One of the main difficulties in doing research has to do with ethics. It is difficult to conduct an experimental trial of drugs with thousands of young people in an ethical manner. One group of young people would have to be designated to ingest or smoke marijuana, and the other group would have to receive a test substance called a placebo. To try and get more up-to-date and accurate data on marijuana use, NIDA came out with two surveys, the National Survey on Drug Use and Health (NSDUH) and the Monitoring the Future Survey. These surveys have been administered each year since the1970s. They have provided data on marijuana use based on information obtained from adolescents and teens. Over the years these studies have followed trends in the attitudes and behavior of middle and high school students when it comes to marijuana use.

WEIGHING THE RISKS

When watching sponsors advertising medications on television, the announcer always states the serious side effects and risks that may happen if a person takes the medication. Written on cigarette packages are warnings about smoking causing cancer. It is right there, front and center on the package. It is important to be aware of risks before using any drug, including marijuana.

Using marijuana can create feelings of euphoria as well as relaxation, but it can also bring on a number of unpleasant side effects. The effects of being high can vary from person to person. After just a few puffs from marijuana, a person's muscles can start relaxing. Then the person may start to giggle. Many people experience changes in their sensory perceptions when they are high. For example, colors may appear brighter. Minutes can seem like hours. The sensory perceptions of hearing and taste can be also be affected by taking marijuana. Some people report that they have a greater appreciation of music while being high. Many people report that they get the munchies after smoking marijuana. This is a type of binge eating. It occurs because the sense of taste is enhanced. Other side effects that can stay in a person well into the next day are red eyes and dry mouth.

Some of the other short-term side effects of marijuana may include:

- Increased heart rate
- Slower perception of time
- Sleepiness
- Loss of motor coordination
- Paranoia (extreme fear)
- Anxiety
- Panic attacks

Teens who smoke marijuana are much more likely to suffer from anxiety and have paranoid thoughts than teens who do not smoke.

ALCOHOL AND MARIJUANA

Many teens have used alcohol and marijuana, two potent drugs, at the same time. The danger of drinking alcohol before smoking marijuana can be severe illness. A side effect called greening out can occur. This means the person may go pale and sweat, feel dizzy, get nauseous, and may start vomiting. But drinking alcohol after smoking marijuana can lead to extremely poor consequences for the person. Usually when a person drinks too much alcohol, their body responds by vomiting. Since marijuana helps prevent vomiting, the body cannot get rid of the toxins created by the alcohol. They can even choke on the vomit they have produced, which could lead to death. Both alcohol and marijuana can create paranoia, anxiety, or terror, allowing the person to make poor choices like getting behind the wheel of a car.

SCHOOL AND WORK PERFORMANCE

According to the 2018 NIDA study, smoking marijuana can have negative effects on attention, memory, and learning for days or even weeks. So if a person is using marijuana daily, their schoolwork will begin to suffer. In a 2018 *Journal of Neurochemistry* study on the effects of marijuana on animals, brain imaging showed marijuana impairs the regions of the brain involved in learning and memory. And according to a 2017 study conducted at the University of

Smoking marijuana on a frequent basis can have a negative effect on memory and attention.

Waterloo, when high school students started smoking regularly, they were less likely to get good grades. The study found that when students started using marijuana at least once a month they were four times more likely to skip class. They were two to four times less likely to complete their homework. Overall teens smoking marijuana frequently were less likely to go to college or university.

BRAIN UNDER CONSTRUCTION

In 2018, NIDA reported that there is enough evidence from animal research and studies on humans to suggest that when young people use marijuana, this can cause long-term or even permanent changes to the brain. One area of major concern is that marijuana can affect a person's IQ. In March 2013, *Psychology Today* reported on a longitudinal study from New Zealand that followed over a thousand people from birth to age thirty-eight. The study participants took IQ tests when they were children and later when they were in their thirties. The results indicated that people who started smoking marijuana in their teens had lower IQ's in their thirties. Those people who started smoking at a younger age most heavily showed the greatest drop in IQ.

MENTAL HEALTH ISSUES

Regular marijuana use in young people has been connected with psychotic symptoms. Psychosis is a pattern of unusual thoughts such as believing the computer is transmitting secret messages when it is not or hearing voices that are not really there. When there is a history of family psychotic disorders, the person is more at risk. According to the Instituto de Medicina Molecular's study in August 2018, using marijuana during adolescence could serve as a trigger for schizophrenia in young people already prone to the disorder. This is not to say that marijuana causes psychosis or schizophrenia but rather it is a risk factor. Some users who had mood disorders and gave up smoking marijuana for a brief time found that their feelings of depression were reduced.

Some young people who smoked marijuana often and over long periods of time reported that they felt their personalities changed. They felt that they had become less outgoing and less social. While many young people become dependent on the feeling of being relaxed when using marijuana, the opposite effect of being anxious can occur. Some long-term marijuana users develop anxiety disorders. They think by taking more marijuana they will get less anxious, but in fact, it can create more anxiety.

BODILY HARM

There are a number of health issues related to marijuana use. Marijuana can irritate the lungs and there can also be a higher risk of lung infections. Regular marijuana smokers are more likely to have a cough that is hard to get rid of. People who smoke marijuana may develop breathing difficulties similar to cigarette smokers. Marijuana smoke is also filled with many of the same chemicals as tobacco smoke. Some of these chemicals are known to cause cancer.

When someone uses marijuana, the THC exits the lungs and enters the bloodstream and then moves throughout the body. According to the NIDA survey, a person's heart rate can increase by as much as fifty beats per minute after using marijuana. This episode can last as long as three hours. Smoking marijuana can actually increase blood flow to one's brain and that makes one's heart work harder. Marijuana smokers who have heart disease can therefore be at higher risk of a heart attack. There is also a possibility of heart rhythm disorders and stroke, even in young people who do not have previous risk factors for heart disease.

People who are heavy smokers of marijuana can develop cannabinoid hyperemesis syndrome, which causes severe gastrointestinal distress.

Marijuana has been used to prevent the feeling of nausea. But some people get the opposite reaction. In April 2018, the *New York Times* reported that cannabinoid hyperemesis syndrome (CHS) is a condition where heavy users can develop symptoms of severe nausea, vomiting, and abdominal pain. There is no data on this illness. But in California and Colorado, which have loosened marijuana laws in recent years, emergency doctors say they are seeing it more often. Doctors say it is difficult to treat. Patients say that they take long, hot showers and baths to help with their

WHAT IS SYNTHETIC MARIJUANA?

Synthetic marijuana, also known as K2 or spice, affects the same parts of the brain that THC does but does not actually contain THC. It is plant material sprayed with chemicals that mimic the high from real marijuana. Synthetic marijuana is unregulated and can be smoked or sold as liquids to be vaporized and inhaled. In April 2018, *Women's Health* reported that at least eighty new synthetic marijuana drugs were identified in one year. These drugs are unsafe. The medical complications from using them can be severe and hard to predict. On August 16, 2018, the *Washington Post* reported that more than seventy people in New Haven, Connecticut, had overdosed on synthetic marijuana. Many were transported to hospitals with symptoms of vomiting, convulsing, and passing out.

The term "K2" is used to describe synthetic marijuana made from dried plant materials sprayed with mind-altering chemicals. People have had life-threatening reactions to K2.

symptoms but after they get out, the symptoms return. Stopping marijuana use appears to be the only cure.

LEGALIZATION CONCERNS

The legalization and regulating marijuana push continues. On one hand, people believe that marijuana has more in common with alcohol and tobacco than it does with harder drugs that are rightly illegal. People also believe that there have been years of unfairly aggressive enforcement for possession of marijuana, especially toward minority populations.

On the other hand, there continues to be concerns about marijuana legalization as there are not enough long-term studies to really evaluate the risks. Legalization may cause an increase of marijuana use in vulnerable populations like adolescents and people suffering mental illnesses. There are concerns that the illegal black market might produce marijuana with even higher rates of THC at lower prices than the government-controlled content. Some people fear that the legalization of marijuana may create problems like addiction down the road. Infrastructure needs to be put into place. Money and resources for drug treatment programs will be necessary.

MYTHS AND FACTS

MYTH: Marijuana is not as popular as other drugs among teens today.

FACT: According to Recovery Village, a drug rehabilitation center, teens use marijuana more than any other illegal drug. Among teens that use drugs, 60 percent use only marijuana.

MYTH: It's easy to quit marijuana. There aren't any withdrawal symptoms.

FACT: Yes there are withdrawal symptoms. Some of these symptoms may include irritability, insomnia, anxiety, and aggressive behavior.

MYTH: Marijuana is not addictive.

FACT: Yes, marijuana can be addictive. Teens may feel the urge to smoke marijuana again and again to get the feeling of being high. Repeated use can lead to addiction. They then may have difficulty stopping, even if they want to stop.

CHAPTER THREE

ADDICTION AND CONSEQUENCES

In the 2017 Monitoring the Future Survey, the results indicated that fewer teens considered marijuana to be harmful compared to previous years. They also saw the drug as a more natural substance and really not a drug. Many teens believe, "It is a plant, so how can it be harmful?" This favorable attitude toward marijuana may be attributed to a number of more positive messages coming through popular culture and the media. On one hand, celebrities like Snoop Dogg and Megan Fox have endorsed marijuana. Rihanna posted pictures of her present for Valentine's Day, a bouquet of marijuana. Justin Timberlake freely admits to smoking marijuana and supports legalization.

On the other hand, a number of celebrities are giving up marijuana. Mark Wahlberg quit smoking marijuana. He reported that he stopped smoking weed for his kids. Natalie Portman also stopped using marijuana once she had children. Many rap songs have lyrics that talk about promoting marijuana, but Chicago-born rapper Common is one artist who has stayed away from using marijuana. He says he has never touched the

Rapper Tyler the Creator, shown performing in Germany in July, 2018, had a negative experience with marijuana and does not use the drug or promote its use by others.

herb. J. Cole admitted that although he used to smoke, he does not anymore. He said he had a phase toward the end of college, but it was never for him. One of the important laws put into place with the legalization of marijuana in Canada is that celebrities are not allowed to endorse it.

Young people describe a number of factors that make them feel attracted to using marijuana. They listen to the lyrics of songs about it. They see people using it in movies and television. They find that using marijuana makes them feel cool. They see the drug as a way of fitting in. They feel that marijuana can help them cope and forget about their problems. They know how to get the drug so it is more available to them.

MARIJUANA ADDICTION

THC, the active ingredient in marijuana, triggers chemical reactions in the brain that control the feelings of relaxation and euphoria. When a person smokes marijuana, the THC passes from the lungs into the bloodstream and then travels to the brain. Marijuana switches on certain receptors in the brain causing symptoms such as mood changes, difficulty thinking, and impaired movement. The more someone smokes marijuana, the more he needs to smoke to experience the same high. It can be a vicious cycle to stop. Users can feel irritable and restless without the drug, so they crave it again. This can lead to marijuana addiction and dependence, which is a state where the person's brain changes because of the THC. The person can go into withdrawal if they stop using marijuana. Sleeping patterns, school work, and outside interests can all be affected. Therefore, marijuana addiction occurs when the body is physically dependent on the drug and craves it even if one experiences negative side effects.

Marijuana can also be psychologically addictive. Teens may feel that they need the drug to meet friends and interact in social situations. Without it, they feel they struggle to be comfortable around other people. Teens who start using marijuana have a higher risk of developing an addiction than adults do. According to the NIDA survey, about 9 percent of people who abuse marijuana will develop an addiction to it over time. The risk rises to 17 percent if they started in their teen years. It rises from 25 to 50 percent in those people who use it every day. Young people who are regular marijuana smokers are more likely to use other illegal drugs. When compared to cigarette smoking and drinking alcohol, marijuana has the fastest rate of leading to a substance abuse disorder among young people.

Marijuana and alcohol have become increasingly available at parties. Combining the two can increase the likelihood of developing alcohol poisoning or suffering from an overdose.

According to the Mayo Clinic, the following symptoms indicate drug addiction to marijuana:

- Cravings for the drug
- Hoarding the drug
- Tolerance for the drug, which then leads to higher doses
- Spending money on marijuana that should go to more essential items
- Not caring about school, work, hobbies, or social activities
- Failed attempts to stop use
- A need to use marijuana daily or several times per day.

HELPING FRIENDS

What should one do if one's friends are using marijuana? There are many ways one can help and support friends. Ultimately, it is the friend who will make the decision to listen to the advice offered. Just telling her about one's concern is a good first step. Assure your friend that she is not alone. Many times the friend is hanging around with others who are getting high. It isn't that these friends cause her to use marijuana, but that they do not encourage her to stop using. It may be difficult for her to remove herself from this other peer group.

CAN A PERSON OVERDOSE ON MARIJUANA?

An overdose occurs when a person uses enough of a drug to produce life-threatening symptoms or death. A person cannot overdose on marijuana. However, a person can experience severe anxiety and panic attacks after using high-potency THC marijuana strains. In some cases, psychotic reactions can include delusions and hallucinations. People can injure themselves because marijuana affects their judgment, perception, and coordination. Dabbing is a form of marijuana use that consists of smoking resins that contain high levels of THC. It is very dangerous, and people have been hospitalized after taking it. Some of the very serious dangerous reaction to

marijuana can include trouble breathing, pale skin color, fast heart rate, and being unresponsive. A person experiencing this requires medical attention immediately. It is best to call 911.

Encouraging your friend to talk to her parents, doctor, the school counselor, or another adult she can trust can lead her in the right direction. When someone you care about makes poor choices, it can be very frustrating and confusing. Listen, encourage, and support.

HIGH OR SLOW, DRIVING WHILE IMPAIRED

In August 2018, the *Globe and Mail* reported that one out of seven people of driving age admitted to driving while high on marijuana. Is it OK to drive if one is high? Alcohol is legal but drunk driving is not. The same rules apply to marijuana. Marijuana may be legal if the doctor has prescribed it for medical reasons or if your state has legalized recreational marijuana but it is illegal to drive impaired. It is a criminal offence when a person is driving a motor vehicle under the influence of alcohol or drugs. The difficulty facing law enforcement now is that there is really not a true test for impairment with marijuana. With alcohol, police can administer a Breathalyzer test. There are also charts that indicate how many alcoholic drinks one can consume over how many hours.

With the legalization of marijuana, more people are driving while high. Marijuana significantly impairs judgment, motor coordination, and reaction time, which can lead to motor vehicle accidents.

There are no charts that tell how many joints or pot brownies are too many before driving. There are pilot projects going on now that are trying to teach police how to test for marijuana drug impairment. In some states they have a Drug Influence Evaluation (DIE), where an expert will look at the drivers' pupil size and check to see if their eyes are red. The expert may also take the people's blood pressure to see if they are impaired. The trouble with doing a urine test is that marijuana can stay in a person's system over a week. The urine test would just confirm that the person has used marijuana but not how much or how recently.

People who smoke marijuana tend to drive slower and leave more distance ahead of them, and the drug's side effects distort their perception of time and space. This means people under the influence of the drug have poor response time, and their judgment is impaired. In March 2018, the *Denver Post* reported that since legalization the number of drivers involved in fatal crashes in Colorado who tested positive for marijuana has risen sharply each year.

CHAPTER FOUR

INTERVENTIONS AND TREATMENT

Many young people start using marijuana and are capable of stopping on their own. But if they require help, there are numerous help lines, addiction centers, printed resources, and websites that a person can contact. In the United States, crisis text is 741 741 and in Canada, Kids Help Line is 1-800-668-6868. Both are available twenty-four hours every day of the week. Religious organizations have clergy that can be trusted to help young people get the resources they require.

A young person who has a marijuana problem or addiction needs to get help. The first step may be to take the young person to their family doctor or pediatrician. The pediatrician may do a drug screening on the person. They may do an individual assessment before recommending next steps. The young person may then be referred to addiction agencies, community health centers, individual therapists, or hospital treatment.

MAKING A REFERRAL

A typical referral process usually starts with an initial phone call. Jewish Addiction Community Services (JACS) reported that their first step in a referral process for young people involved in marijuana is usually when a parent calls in. The parent is very concerned because their son or daughter is displaying behaviors that are worrisome. Some of these behaviors may include not doing well in school or skipping classes altogether. Their child is not obeying curfews and is displaying a lot of anger and moodiness. He may have stopped going to his after-school activities like playing hockey or basketball. Parents may suspect something is going on as they start seeing their child hanging around with friends that appear to be high. They may report that their child is choosing to

Marijuana use can put a strain on the relationship between a teen and his parents, but there are organizations that can help family members communicate in more productive ways.

TWELVE QUESTIONS FROM MARIJUANA ANONYMOUS

Marijuana Anonymous (MA) holds regional meetings in many states to help people stop using marijuana. It uses the twelve steps of recovery founded by Alcoholics Anonymous as it has proven to have great success. MA uses the following twelve questions. If one answers yes to any of the questions, MA recommends that the person seek help by attending their meetings.

- Has smoking marijuana stopped being fun?
- Do you ever get high alone?
- Is it hard for you to imagine a life without marijuana?
- Do you find that your friends are determined by your marijuana use?
- Do you use marijuana to avoid dealing with your problems?
- Do you smoke marijuana to cope with your feelings?
- Does your marijuana use let you live in a privately defined world?
- Have you ever failed to keep promises you made about cutting down or controlling your use of marijuana?
- Has your use of marijuana caused problems with memory, concentration, or motivation?
- When your stash is nearly empty, do you feel anxious or worried about how to get more?
- Do you plan your life around your marijuana use?
- Have friends or relatives ever complained that your using is damaging your relationship with them?

be with these friends and not with family. Parents may have found drug paraphernalia like marijuana joints or bongs hidden away in their child's bedroom.

Parents phone the agency because they need help and do not know where to turn to. JACS sets up a meeting with the parent to gather information and after the intake, a session for the family, including the child, is scheduled. JACS conducts individual and group sessions and has had great success through their programming in getting young people to make better choices and get off drugs. Their website for helpful resources is jacstoronto.org.

MARIJUANA ADDICTION TREATMENT

Young people who start using marijuana have a higher risk of developing an addiction than those who start using as adults. Marijuana addiction can be successfully treated if addressed with proper treatment.

Therapy is one of the main treatments for marijuana addiction. The goal of therapy is to provide young people with techniques so that they can either avoid or cope with triggers that lead to using marijuana. Therapy can teach the young person problem-solving skills so they can live their life without dependence on drugs. Therapists work with young people to help them know how to refuse drugs when offered to them. The programs teach them strategies so they will not relapse. These therapy sessions might be individual or in groups. The National Council on Alcoholism and Drug Dependence (NCADD) reports that more young people enter treatment with a primary diagnosis of marijuana dependency than for all other illegal drugs combined.

THERAPIES FOR MARIJUANA ADDICTION

COGNITIVE BEHAVIORAL THERAPY

In cognitive behavioral therapy (CBT) the person learns to identify and then try and correct problematic behaviors. CBT helps people become aware of inaccurate or negative thinking so they can view challenging situations more clearly and respond to them in a more effective way. People develop effective coping strategies rather than taking drugs. Some of the techniques therapists use are exploring the positive and negative consequences of continued marijuana use. For example, the teen's grades in school have fallen sharply since she is smoking marijuana every day.

The therapist helps the teen become more aware of situations where she might be put at risk. If she knows that an event is coming and drugs will be used, she does not go. The therapist works with the person to develop strategies for coping with her cravings for the drug. The good news is that research indicates that these skills that the teen has learned will stay with her after treatment.

A trained therapist can help someone concerned about his or her dependence on marijuana develop positive coping strategies to deal with life's stressors without needing to smoke pot.

CONTINGENCY MANAGEMENT

Contingency management (CM) refers to a type of behavioral therapy in which the person is reinforced or rewarded for evidence of positive change. Some of the reinforcers are vouchers that can be exchanged for goods or an opportunity to win prizes. Money has also been used as a reinforcer. One example of a positive change that a person can strive toward is having a clear urine test that does not contain evidence of marijuana. The goal of the program is that the desire to keep clean and not use marijuana will continue when the rewards are removed.

MOTIVATIONAL ENHANCEMENT THERAPY

Motivational enhancement therapy (MET) is a treatment that helps people set personal goals that they want to achieve. Counselors work with the person to help him meet his goals. For example, a therapist may ask, "What do you think you can do about your problem with marijuana?" The therapist then works with the person to create a change plan. This plan outlines steps the person will take in order to achieve his goal.

GROUP COUNSELING

Group counseling is a popular way for teens to receive therapy. It takes place in a safe environment, where there is confidentiality. The counselors are trained and have an understanding of what the teens are going through. Some of the themes that may be discussed in group therapy are:

- Relationships
- Diet and exercise
- Family dynamics
- Making better choices
- Education on drugs and how it affects the user

Teens who exercise on a regular basis are less likely to smoke cigarettes or abuse marijuana than their more sedentary peers.

FAMILY COUNSELING

A young person addicted to marijuana is not all alone. She shares a home with her family members. Altogether they can learn strategies to help each other. Family therapy can improve the family relationships through:

- Developing a supportive environment
- Creating honesty
- Developing trust
- Reducing stress and tension within the family
- Bringing the family together after a crisis

INDIVIDUAL THERAPY

Individual therapy (sometimes called "psychotherapy" or "counseling") is a process in which a young person works with a trained therapist one-on-one. The therapy is done in a safe, confidential, and caring office. The therapist helps the person work through his feelings and behaviors. The therapist also helps the young person work on his self esteem.

MEDICAL INTERVENTION

There does not appear to be any medications for treating marijuana addiction, but it is an area that is being researched. There have been clinical trials of several drugs to find out if they can relieve withdrawal symptoms, including antianxiety drugs, antidepressants, and sleep aids.

DETOX

If a person has a severe addiction to marijuana, a detox program may be recommended. Detox means to rid the body of toxic or unhealthy substances. Detox programs are short-term forms of treatment that help the person safely withdraw from marijuana. At the same time the person is given medical care and support. Patients often transfer to an inpatient or outpatient program following the completion of their detox program.

INPATIENT AND OUTPATIENT TREATMENT

Many states offer inpatient marijuana addiction rehabilitation. Teens live at the rehabilitation center full time, where they are provided a supportive, drug-free place. They get intensive individual therapy as well as group therapy. As they make progress, they step down in levels of care, eventually leading to outpatient support. Outpatient support means the teen can live at home and travel to the center as needed. These centers usually come with a cost. Some may be partially covered under insurance.

After treatment, the person should connect with an aftercare support group. Having a network of other people that have a similar journey with drug addiction allows a person to find immediate help when the temptation to use becomes strong. Therapy is a very individual choice. What works for one person may not necessarily be the therapy of choice for another person. It is very important to feel comfortable with the therapy and therapist that one chooses.

CHAPTER FIVE

MAKING BETTER CHOICES

Adolescents and teens gravitate to other young people. Many prefer to chat or text with their peers and follow their advice. Peer groups are likely to influence a person's beliefs and behavior. Peer pressure is when words or actions of a peer group make people feel that in order to be part of the "in" group they must act and do what the peer group does. Peer pressure can be a bad thing when it leads to making poor choices or developing bad habits. But peer pressure can also lead to positive habits and making better choices. When it comes to marijuana, teens are very susceptible to their peer group. Teens tend to keep smoking if their friends do it, but if their friends are not smoking marijuana, they mostly do not use it.

PARENTAL GUIDANCE

Most parents are surprised to learn that they can influence their children when it comes to attitudes about drugs. Teens need to hear from their parents consistently how risky marijuana is and how the drug can damage their lives if they start and continue using drugs. Adolescents trust the messages from their parents because it is coming from people they respect and love. By staying involved with their children, knowing what their children are doing, and setting limits with clear rules and consequences, parents can help their children avoid drugs. Parents need to ask their children what they know about marijuana. The parent can give facts, not myths. The website drugfreekidscanada.org reports that teenagers that are involved in constructive, adult-supervised activities are less likely to use drugs than other teens.

It takes a lot of courage to tell a friend how her frequent marijuana use is having a negative effect on your relationship.

SCHOOL RULES

Schools are trying hard to create safe environments for their students. Schools receive accurate marijuana information as part of their curriculum. Under the direction of school boards and principals, teachers plan units of study on marijuana. They develop a variety of teaching approaches and select good resources. They want to prepare students to enjoy healthy living and to discourage and prevent drug use among their students.

Scholastic has a website (http://headsup.scholastic.com/teachers/marijuana-facts-lesson) that provides students with worksheets to complete based on what they have learned about marijuana from their school's curriculum. One of their assignments is to create a twenty second public service announcement for TV or the Web that will give viewers facts about marijuana or important health information related to marijuana use. Their goal is to give their peers the information they need to make informed decisions based on facts. They can use animation, voice-over with pictures, interviews, plays, or other creative activities. They then present their broadcast to the class. NIDA also has a website (https://teens.drugabuse.gov/teachers/lessonplans) that provides teachers and students with lesson plans and activities about marijuana. The aim of these exercises is to try and encourage learning about the effects of marijuana in an informative and fun way.

While teachers do not provide direct counseling and addiction services, they can see behavior changes in their students. They can see that their student has red and glassy eyes. They can tell that their student's grades have dropped, and the student is not completing homework. They can refer their

As part of the school curriculum, teachers and counselors educate students about the dangers of alcohol and drugs, including marijuana, so teens can make informed decisions about their lives.

students to counseling in or outside of the school with parental permission.

AVOIDING TEMPTATION

It can be difficult to avoid the temptation of taking marijuana. It is easier to avoid situations where you may face temptation. When you know there will be drugs at a party, and no adult supervision, don't attend. If a group of peers go out at lunch to smoke marijuana, get involved in a supervised lunch activity. If a group is going to hang out at a mall after school, and they will eventually start smoking marijuana, come up with an excuse to go home instead. When a joint is passed around, avoid smoking it. Just walk away or just say it is a personal choice not to smoke. Joining an after school activity like a supervised sports team creates a peer group that doesn't focus on getting high. As difficult as it may be, finding friends that respect one's attitude to saying no to marijuana is a positive thing.

Making the decision to stop using marijuana can be a challenge. First of all, you have to admit that there is a problem and have a commitment to quitting. Get rid of all paraphernalia like cigarette papers, lighters, and bongs. Drop any identity that one has maintained as a marijuana user. For example, on social media, get rid of the name "Bud" or "Green Goddess." It is really important to avoid any places or people that may trigger marijuana use. If you find yourself in a risky environment, be willing to leave the situation right away. A strong and understanding support network is needed to stay off marijuana. Rely on peers and family who will support and respect confidentiality. Know that withdrawal symptoms do occur. Take it one day at a time.

FEELING EMPOWERED

Growing up has many challenges. There are so many paths one can take on one's journey. There are crossroads that one will encounter. Marijuana may be legalized for medical and recreational purposes in one's state.

SEARCHING FOR HELP

During high school, she always looked around and felt she wanted to be part of the popular group. At the beginning of grade twelve, she started hanging out with a peer group that liked to smoke marijuana behind the building at school during lunch hours. She liked how it made her feel. She felt like she fit in. Although smoking marijuana began at lunch, she started to use marijuana after school and on weekends. She was always a decent student but her grades started to drop. After three months of using marijuana every day, her parents approached her and cried and begged her to seek help. They went into family counseling with a social worker experienced with drug addictions. She became angry, then embarrassed. Finally, she admitted she did have a problem and needed the help. The social worker helped her set goals. Her parents were given guidelines to follow. Her family supported her as she went through her withdrawal symptoms. It was the hardest work she had ever done. Even now, when she gets a whiff of the marijuana smell, it creates cravings. But to graduate was the goal she had set for herself, and she was successful.

But remember, recreational marijuana is illegal if one is underage. People need a prescription from a qualified doctor to get medical marijuana. In places where marijuana is legal, it is sold in authorized stores and is government controlled. If marijuana is purchased in unauthorized places, it can be laced with dangerous drugs.

What choices can a teen make? It may be confusing to receive messages endorsing marijuana from popular culture, whether it is a TV show, a chart-topping song, or a post on a website. To live a life free of marijuana requires a strong choice to say no and continue to say no to unhealthy and destructive behaviors. If one has already tried marijuana then the decision to discontinue may also be difficult. Choosing the path that will lead to a healthy lifestyle will benefit you now and as you make your way toward adulthood. You are never alone. There are lots of people trained to help you on your journey. Just ask.

10 GREAT QUESTIONS TO ASK AN ADDICTION SPECIALIST

1. Is marijuana addictive?
2. Can you smoke marijuana and drive?
3. How long does marijuana remain in your system?
4. Does smoking marijuana every day mean I am an addict?
5. What is the difference between recreational and medical marijuana?
6. I know someone my age who seems addicted, what does one do?
7. Can marijuana lead to stronger and more addictive drugs?
8. Is smoking marijuana as bad as smoking cigarettes?
9. Does marijuana affect people differently?
10. Can you mix marijuana with other prescription medicine?

GLOSSARY

addiction Repeated involvement with a substance or activity despite the substantial harm it causes.

anxiety A nervous disorder characterized by a state of excessive uneasiness and apprehension.

black market The illegal, unregulated sale of goods or services.

blunt A hollowed-out cigar filled with marijuana.

bong A device used for smoking various substances, but most commonly marijuana.

chemotherapy A treatment for cancer with (frequently toxic) chemicals.

criminalized Turning (an activity) into a criminal offense by making it illegal.

epilepsy A common brain disorder characterized by recurrent seizures.

euphoria A feeling of excitement, happiness, and well- being.

infrastructure The basic structure or features of a system or organization.

joint A cigarette made from marijuana or from marijuana mixed with tobacco.

mood disorder When one is extremely sad, empty, or irritable (depressed) or when one may have periods of depression alternating with being excessively happy (mania).

multiple sclerosis A chronic disease that attacks the central nervous system.

placebo A substance that has no therapeutic effect and is used as a control in testing new drugs.

resin A dark to light brown substance that is scraped off the surface of the cannabis plant and pressed into a solid lump.

schizophrenia A mental disorder characterized by abnormal social behavior and failure to understand reality.

sensory Connected with the physical senses of touch, smell, taste, hearing, and sight.

THC The main mind-altering ingredient found in the cannabis plant.

vaping Inhaling and exhaling vapor from an electronic cigarette or similar device.

withdrawal The negative physical effects of giving up a substance or drug.

FOR MORE INFORMATION

American Council for Drug Education (ACDE)
164 West 74th Street
New York, NY 10023
(800) 488-DRUG [3784]
Website: http://www.acde.org

The American Council for Drug Education is a substance abuse prevention and education agency that develops programs and materials based on the most current scientific research on drug use and its impact on society. Their website provides information about the signs and effects of substance abuse.

American Medical Association (AMA)
AMA Plaza
330 N. Wabash Avenue, Suite 39300
Chicago, IL 60611
(800) 621-8335
Website: http://www.ama-assn.org
Twitter: @AmerMedicalAssn
YouTube: American Medical Association (AMA)
The AMA provides up-to-date information and strategies to assist doctors and patients on issues such as medical marijuana.

Canadian Centre on Substance Use and Addiction (CCSA)
75 Albert Street, Suite 500
Ottawa, ON K1P 5E7
Canada

(833) 235-4048
(613) 235-4048
Website: http://www.ccsa.ca
Twitter: @CCSACanada
CCSA works with its partners to address issues related to substance abuse and addiction that affect the health and safety of all Canadians. It offers a comprehensive guide on how to talk to youth about marijuana, which is available for download.

Canadian Institutes of Health Research (CIHR)
160 Elgin Street, 9th Floor
Address Locator 4809A
Ottawa ON K1A 0W9
Canada
(613) 954-1968
Toll Free: (888) 603-4178
Website: http://www.support@cihr-irsc.gc.ca
Twitter: @CIHR_IRSC
CIHR is Canada's federal funding agency for health research. They fund research on topics like marijuana addiction.

National Association of Addiction Treatment Providers (NAATP)
Chancery Building
1120 Lincoln Street, Suite 1303
Denver, CO 80203
(888) 574-1008
Website: http://www.info@naatp.org
Facebook:

@nationalassociationofaddictiontreatmentproviders
Twitter: @NAATPMarv
The mission of NAATP is to provide leadership, advocacy, training, and member support services to ensure the availability and highest quality of addiction treatment.

National Institute on Drug Abuse (NIDA)
Office of Science Policy and Communications
Public Information and Liaison Branch
6001 Executive Boulevard
Room 5213, MSC 9561
Bethesda, MD 20892
(301) 443-1124
Website: https://www.drugabuse.gov/publications/drugfacts/marijuana
Twitter: Twitter@NIDANews
NIDA is a great resource for parents, students, and teachers. It contains the latest science-based information about the health effects and consequences of drug use and addiction. It provides resources for talking with children about the impact of drug use on health.

Substance Abuse and Mental Health Services Administration (SAMHSA)
5600 Fishers Lane
Rockville, MD 20757
877-SAMHSA-7 (877-726-4727)
800-487-4889 (TTY)
Website: https://samhsa.gov

Twitter: @samhsagov
YouTube: SAMHSA
The Substance Abuse and Mental Health Services Administration (SAMHSA) is the agency within the US Department of Health and Human Services that leads public health efforts to advance the behavioral health of the nation. SAMHSA's mission is to reduce the impact of substance abuse and mental illness on America's communities.

FOR FURTHER READING

Barcott, Bruce. *Weed the People.* New York, NY: Time, 2015.

Baughman, Michael. *Growers Market: A Novel of Free Enterprise in Marijuana Country.* New York, NY: Skyhorse Publishing, 2015.

Blacks, Michael. *Cannabis Pharmacy: The Practical Guide to Medical Marijuana Revised and Updated.* New York, NY: Black Dog & Leventhal, 2017.

Brown Hamilton, Tracy. *I am Addicted to Drugs. Now What?* New York, NY: Rosen Publishing, 2017.

Buntin, Julie. *Marlena: A Novel.* New York, NY: Henry Holt and Company, 2017.

Currie–McGhee, Leanne. *Teens and Marijuana.* San Diego, CA: Reference Point Press, 2015

Esposito, Jim. *High Fliers.* Scotts Valley, CA: CreateSpace, 2016.

Hudak, John. *Marijuana, A Short History.* Washington, DC : Brookings Institution Press, 2016.

Jenson, Frances, and Amy Ellis Nutt. *The Teenage Brain.* New York, NY: Harper Collins Publishing, 2015.

Martin, Alyson, and Nushin Rashidian. *A New Leaf: The End of Cannabis Prohibition.* New York, NY: The New Press, 2014.

Van Gundy, Karen T., and Michael S., Staunton. *Marijuana Examining the Facts.* Santa Barbara, CA: ABC-CLIO Company, 2017.

BIBLIOGRAPHY

Brophy Marcus, Mary. "What Is Synthetic Marijuana—And Is It Safe? I Don't Want Anyone to Think These Substances are Anything like Marijuana." *Women's Health*, April 2, 2018. https://www.womenshealthmag.com.

De Salvo, Robert. "Celebrities Who Quit Smoking Weed / Famous People Who Stopped Using Marijuana." *Ranker*. Retrieved September 12, 2018. https://www.ranker.com/list/celebrities-who-quit-smoking-weed/robert-desalvo.

Gerstein, Josh, and Lima Cristiano. "Sessions Announces End to Policy that Allowed Legal Pot to Flourish." *Politico*, January 4, 2018.https://www.politico.com.

Gumbiner, Jann. "Marijuana and Intelligence. Does Long-Term Use of Cannabis Make You Dumber?" *Psychology Today*, March 19, 2013. https://www.psychologytoday.com/ca/blog/the-teenage-mind/201303/marijuana-and-intelligence.

Hager, Mike. "One in Seven Cannabis Users Admits They Consumed Drug Then Drove Statscan Says." *Globe and Mail*, August 14, 2018. https://www.theglobeandmail.com.

Kenter, Peter. "First of its Kind Study Suggests Cannabis as an Alternative to Opioids for Pain Management." *National Post*, September 8, 2018. https://www.nationalpost.com.

Migoya, David. "Traffic Fatalities Linked to Marijuana are up Sharply in Colorado. Is Legalization to Blame?" *Denver Post*, March 26, 2018. https://www.denverpost.com.

Mouro, Francisco. "Chronic, Intermittent Treatment with a Cannabinoid Receptor Agonist Impairs Recognition Memory and Brain Network Functional Connectivity." *Journal of Neurochemistry*, July10, 2018. https://www.natap.org.

National Council on Alcoholism and Drug Dependence. "Marijuana." April 26, 2015. https://www.ncadd.org/about-addiction/drugs/marijuana.

National Institute on Drug Abuse. "DrugFacts: Marijuana." June 2018. https://www.drugabuse.gov/publications/drugfacts/marijuana.

National Institute on Drug Abuse. "Monitoring the Future." December 14, 2017. https://www.drugabuse.gov/related-topics/trends-statistics/monitoring-future.

National Survey on Drug Use and Health (NSDUH), The. "Welcome to the National Survey on Drug Use and health." January 1, 2018. https://nsduhweb.rti.org/respweb/homepage.cfm.

New York Law Journal. "Manhattan DA Moves to Throw Out More than 3000 Old Pot Convictions." September 12, 2018. https://www.law.com/newyorklawjournal.

Rabin, Roni Caryn. "A Perplexing Marijuana Side Effect Relieved by Hot Showers." *New York Times*, April 5, 2018. https://www.nytimes.com/2018/04/05/well/a-perplexing-marijuana-side-effect-relieved-by-hot-showers.html.

Schmidt, Samantha. "It is Taking People Out: More than 70 people Overdose on K2 in a Single Day in New Haven." *Washington Post*, August 16, 2018. https://www.washingtonpost.com./news/morning-mix/wp/2018/08/16/it-is-taking-people-out-more-than

-70-people-overdose-on-k2-in-a-single-day-in-new-haven/?utm_term=.b16eaed25360.

Sebastião, Ana. "How Cannabis and Cannabis-Based Drugs Harm the Brain." Instituto de Medicina Molecular, August 13, 2018. https://www.sciencedaily.com.

University of Waterloo. "Marijuana Use Tied to Poorer School Performance." *Waterloo News,* May 11, 2017. https://uwaterloo.ca/news/news/marijuana-use-tied-poorer-school-performance.

Williams, Timothy. "Marijuana Arrests Outnumber Those for Violent Crimes, Study Finds." *New York Times*, October 13, 2016. https://www.nytimes.com/2016/10/13/us/marijuana-arrests.html.

Winstock, Dr. Adam. "Global Drug Survey 2017." May 24, 2017. https://www.globaldrugsurvey.com.

Zezima, Katie. "Study: Legal Marijuana Could Generate More than $132 billion in Federal Tax Revenue and 1 Million Jobs." *Chicago Tribune*, January 10, 2018. http://www.chicagotribune.com.

INDEX

ABOUT THE AUTHOR

Dr. Sandra Giddens has been an educational consultant and coordinator for school boards in Toronto. She has a doctorate in special education. She focuses on helping and supporting students who have behavior issues to make better choices in their lives. Giddens volunteers at the Hospital for Sick Children in Toronto. She is an author of a number of books for Rosen Publishing.

PHOTO CREDITS

Cover L. Robindro Singh/EyeEm/Getty Images; back cover photo by marianna armata/Moment/Getty Images; p. 5 Bloomberg/Getty Images; pp. 6, 16, 26, 34, 44 Norman Posselt/Getty Images; p. 7 Lifestyle discover/Shutterstock .com; p. 8 Peter Simon/Archive Photos/Getty Images; p. 10 william casey/Shutterstock.com; p. 11 Robyn Beck/AFP/ Getty Images; p. 13 sirtravelalot/Shutterstock.com; p. 18 file404/Shutterstock.com; p. 19 MIXA/Getty Images; p. 22 Daisy Daisy/Shutterstock.com; p. 23 The Washington Post/ Getty Images; p. 27 © AP Images; p. 29 Lisa Peardon/The Image Bank/Getty Images; p. 32 Doug Menuez/Photodisc/ Getty Images; p. 35 Nancy Ney/Photodisc/Getty Images; p. 39 Tetra Images/Getty Images; p. 41 Tirachard Kumtanom/ Shutterstock.com; p. 45 Westend61/Getty Images; p. 47 Monkey Business Images/Shutterstock.com.

Design: Michael Moy; Layout: Tahara Anderson;
Editor: Jennifer Landau; Photo Researcher: Sherri Jackson